monster Chronicles

ZOMBIES

Stephen Krensky

Lerner Publications Company · Minneapolis

Lerner Publications Company
A division of Lerner Publishing Group, Inc.
241 First Avenue North
Minneapolis, MN 55401 U.S.A.

Website address: www.lernerbooks.com

Library of Congress Cataloging-in-Publication Data

Krensky, Stephen.
    Zombies / by Stephen Krensky.
        p.   cm. — (Monster chronicles)
    Includes bibliographical references and index.
    ISBN: 978-0-8225-6759-2 (lib. bdg. : alk. paper)
    1. Zombies—Juvenile literature. I. Title.
    GR581.K74 2008
    398'.45—dc22   2006101485

Manufactured in the United States of America
1 2 3 4 5 6 - JR - 13 12 11 10 09 08

TABLE OF CONTENTS

1

BACK FROM THE DEAD

Imagine a dead body stumbling toward you in the dark. Its skin color is gray. Its eyes are glazed. The flesh is rotting off its bones. It lurches forward with arms outstretched. What would you do?

Would you scream? Would you run away? Would you faint?

Whatever you do, you would be smart to do it fast. The dead body is a zombie. Legend says that if it catches you, you're doomed. A zombie doesn't want to be your friend. A zombie wants to make you its next victim. It might even eat you. Even if you run or hide, you're not necessarily safe. The zombie will never stop looking for you. According to lore, zombies are always on the hunt, always looking for victims.

WHAT SORT OF MONSTER?

Zombies are dead people said to have been brought back to life. As monsters go, they have few equals. They're ugly, they're scary, and their favorite time for wandering around is the middle of the night.

Zombies wear the clothes they were wearing when they were buried. They don't care about stains or tears, not to mention fashions.

What do zombies do? Actually, the list of things zombies don't do is much longer than the list of things they are said to do. Zombies don't sleep because they never get tired. They don't breathe, and they don't feel pain. They don't remember anything about their lives before they were zombies.

Zombies are said to be hard to stop. You can chop off a zombie's arm, and the zombie will still come after you. Even chopping off a zombie's legs won't stop the attack. Zombies don't mind heat or cold. In tales, they keep going and going.

Zombies moan and groan. But they do not talk. That's because their brains have been wiped clean. They don't know who they used to be while alive—and they don't care. Becoming a zombie is never the zombie's idea. Instead, someone else—or an outside force—brings the zombie back from the dead. Whoever or whatever it is, that force is in charge. A zombie is just a servant or slave of somebody or something else.

The word *zombie* comes from the Kimbundu (an African language) word *nzumbe*, meaning "ghost."

In *The Ghost Breakers*, a film made in 1940, a zombie chases Mary Carter, played by Paulette Goddard *(left)*, through a haunted house.

Stories tell of people brought back from the dead and forced to do hard work. Zombies don't eat or sleep, and they don't need money, so they're easy workers to please.

Another name for zombies is the undead.

A few zombies are said to be harmless. They wait around for orders. They keep busy with farm chores and household errands. They have no special strengths or powers. They do what they're told. When they're finished, they move on to the next assigned task.

In some cases (depending on which horror movie you watch), people killed by zombies turn into zombies themselves.

Zombies in other tales cause trouble. They like to rip apart their victims and eat human flesh. In the quest for that next meal, they are relentless. They are very strong, although not very fast. But they keep on coming. They overwhelm everything in their paths. If you happen to be in a zombie's way—well, you won't be for long.

A SIMPLE MONSTER

Compared to other monsters, zombies aren't glamorous. The vampire Dracula is suave and sophisticated. Originally, he was a rich nobleman.

The famous vampire character named Dracula resembles a Romanian prince named Vlad Tepes (left). He lived in the 1400s and was known for his cruel and violent treatment of his enemies.

Mummies are also high-class monsters. Before they were mummies, many of them were Egyptian kings and high priests. But zombies are much simpler. They have no big goals or ambitions. Unlike some monsters, they aren't evil masterminds or sneaky villains. Zombies don't want to rule the world.

In ancient Egypt, important people were mummified for religious reasons. Only later did mummies become scary monsters.

A zombie's family and friends might be sad. But zombies aren't sad about being zombies. They don't even know who they are. They don't show much in the way of feelings. They do as they're told and leave it at that.

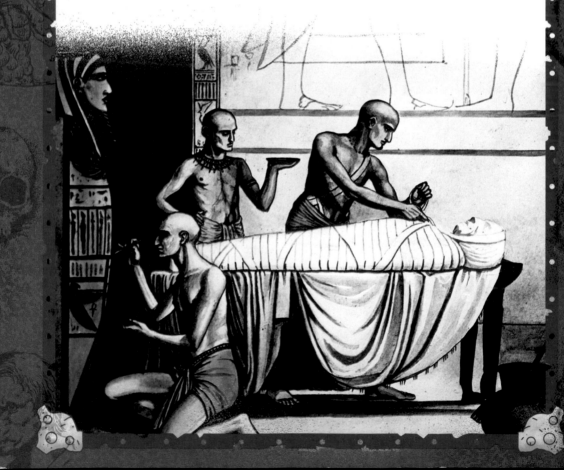

The monster Frankenstein is named after a doctor who built a monster from dead body parts in Mary Shelley's 1818 book *Frankenstein*. This book cover is from the late 1800s.

MONSTERS FROM THE DEAD

In addition to zombies, several other fictional monsters are people who also have come back from the dead. These monsters include vampires, mummies, and ghosts. Frankenstein walks like a zombie (so do mummies). His movements are stiff and mechanical. The story goes that he was created from dead body parts. But unlike zombies and others monsters, he was never a single living being.

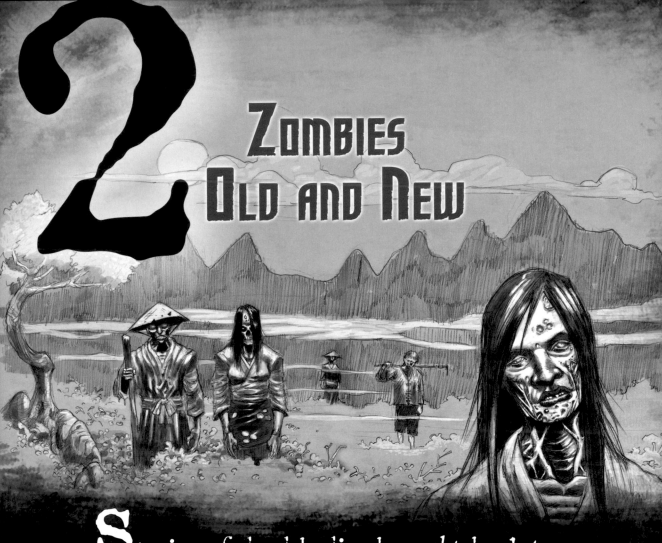

2 ZOMBIES OLD AND NEW

Stories of dead bodies brought back to life have existed for thousands of years—although the creatures weren't called zombies then. In the Middle East, ancient peoples told a story called the Epic of Gilgamesh. In one part of the tale, a goddess named Ishtar gets angry. She threatens to bring the dead back to eat the living.

The Bible tells about a man named Lazarus. According to the story, four days after Lazarus dies, Jesus raises him from the dead. Lazarus is not a zombie, though. He has all his memories, and his life goes back to normal after his return from the dead.

The Epic of Gilgamesh was first written on clay tablets *(left)* almost five thousand years ago.

Other returned-from-the-dead figures are not so lucky. In Chinese myths, zombies are called the Kuang Shi. They have human bodies but no free will or independent thought. They are mindless soldiers who follow the commands of an evil leader.

The Bible does not explain what happened to Lazarus (in tomb) after he was raised from the dead. Most people assume that he went back to a normal life with his family.

In some Chinese myths, zombies are dead people who die far from home. They must walk back to their home villages before they can rest in peace.

In Scandinavian legends, zombies are called *draugrs*. Unlike most zombies, draugrs have distinct personalities. During life they were said to be fierce warriors called Vikings. After death, these Vikings were not content to lie in their graves. They came back to attack the living. For ordinary Scandinavians, it was scary enough to worry about any dead person coming back to life. But worrying about a dead warrior with greater-than-normal strength was even worse. It took a brave hero to defeat a draugr. The hero had to wrestle the draugr before cutting off its head. To make sure the draugr never returned, people in legends would burn its body and scatter the ashes at sea.

During the Middle Ages (about A.D. 500 to 1500), English people told stories about revenants. They were spirits who rose from the grave to haunt the living. During life, many revenants were said to have been criminals. After death they continued their evil ways. They killed people and spread sickness. To stop a revenant, townspeople believed they had to dig up the dead body, remove its heart, and cut off its head.

In this folktale illustration from 1910, the pale young woman *(left)* is a revenant. She returns to her family and finds that they have forgotten about her.

Do You Voodoo?

Zombies have never been confined to just one place. Zombie stories come from all over the world—Europe, Asia, North America, Africa, and the Middle East. But in the past two hundred years, the most common place to find zombies has been Haiti. Haiti is part of an island called Hispaniola. The island is in the Caribbean Sea.

The first people to live in Haiti were Native Americans. In the 1500s, settlers from Spain, France, England, and other European nations moved to Haiti. The Europeans fought among themselves for control of Haiti. Eventually, the French took over.

Haiti was once covered by a lush, tropical rain forest. European settlers cut most of the trees to make way for farms.

French settlers in Haiti bought slaves to tend their homes and farms. The slaves came mostly from West Africa. The African slaves practiced ancient religions. But in Haiti, masters forced their slaves to follow the Christian religion. The slaves did not forget their old religions, however. They mixed their new Christian beliefs with their old African ones. One of these ancient African beliefs was voodoo.

Voodoo is a complex religious tradition. People who practice voodoo believe in a single god and many spirits. Some of these spirits are good. Others

Starting in the 1700s, tens of thousands of slaves were brought to Haiti every year. In 1804 the slaves revolted *(below)* against their French masters . The slaves declared their freedom, and Haiti became independent from France.

are evil. Voodoo also has good and evil priests, or sorcerers. The good priests use their special powers to help people. The evil priests are called *bokors*. They are the ones who make zombies.

Bokors create zombies for one of three reasons. The first reason is for cheap labor. After all, zombies work without complaining. They never ask for a raise or better working conditions. In fact, they work for free. The second reason to turn somebody into a zombie is for revenge. If someone has wronged you, turning that person into a zombie probably seems like a just punishment. The third reason is for power. An evil person might want a zombie army to control people and places. All these motives keep the bokors in business.

This Haitian woman is taking part in a voodoo ritual. People dance and chant to pounding drums, inviting spirits to communicate through them.

HOW TO MAKE A ZOMBIE

Making a zombie is complicated. To turn someone into a zombie, a bokor must take possession of that person's soul. In voodoo, there are two methods. In the first, the bokor rides backward on a horse to the victim's house. Once there, the bokor sucks out the victim's soul through a door or window. Without a soul, the victim soon dies. After the victim is buried, the bokor secretly returns to the grave and opens it. The bokor then passes the soul under the victim's nose for a moment—just long enough to wake up the body. The bokor then leads the body away.

The second method involves magical ingredients. The bokor begins with a thunderstone, a rock that has been buried underground for a year. Other ingredients include human bones, a puffer fish, a sea snake, toads, spiders, and a few insects. The bokor buries some of the ingredients

Men dressed as zombies participate in a holiday parade in Santo Domingo. The city is in the Dominican Republic on the island of Hispaniola, where people also practice voodoo.

underground for a few days, burns all the ingredients in a fire, and then grinds them into a powder. The powder is poison. For the poison to work, it must be absorbed though the victim's skin. So the bokor places the poison in a spot where the victim is likely to walk barefoot. Once the poison takes effect, the victim will seem to weaken and die. However, a spark of life remains. Once the body is buried, the bokor comes along and digs it up.

Once a zombie has been created, the bokor must keep the zombie obedient. So bokors feed zombies a paste, made from a plant called zombie's cucumber. Chemicals in a zombie's cucumber keep zombies in a weakened condition, so they are easy to order around.

In the United States, zombie's cucumber is called jimsonweed.

ZOMBIE PREVENTION

According to the tradition of Haitian voodoo, people can take precautions to make sure a deceased loved one doesn't become a zombie. They can bury the body under heavy stones to make it more difficult to dig up. They can watch over the loved one's grave for thirty-six hours. After this time, the death is final and a bokor can no longer turn the dead body into a zombie. To eliminate all doubt of a body being turned into a zombie, people can cut off its head.

BAD PUBLIC RELATIONS

Outside Haiti, voodoo has gotten a bad reputation, mostly because of films. Horror movies such as *Voodoo Bloodbath* (1964) and *Curse of the Voodoo* (1965) have presented unrealistic and negative pictures of voodoo. Zombie movies have also given voodoo a bad name. In reality, voodoo is similar to many world religions. Called animist religions, these faiths involve spirit worship *(above)* and ancestor worship.

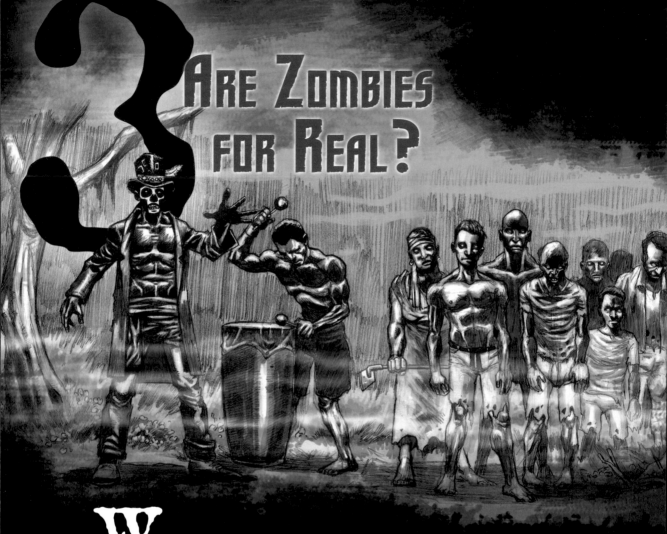

?Are Zombies for Real?

When it comes to magical things, some people are skeptics, or nonbelievers. They doubt the existence of zombies and other fantastic creatures. They don't believe in vampires or unicorns or even the tooth fairy. There is no such thing, they say, as a dead person brought back to life. It's just not possible.

The skeptics have common sense on their side. Yet some people tell stories about actually seeing zombies. These are not dramatic tales of adventure. They are not legends or horror stories. But they leave us wondering: is it possible that zombies are real?

STEPPING OUT OF THE SHADOWS

In Haiti, people have told stories about zombies for centuries. At first, most Haitians did not write down their observations about zombies. However, in the 1900s, visitors to Haiti did write about zombies. These writings sparked interest in zombies in the United States.

William Seabrook *(left)* popularized the word *zombie* in his book *The Magic Island* (1929).

William Seabrook was an author from the United States. He visited Haiti in the 1920s. A Haitian farmer promised to show Seabrook some real zombies. Seabrook was eager to see them. He was not so eager after he saw his first zombie, however. "The [zombie's] eyes were the worst," Seabrook wrote. "It was not my imagination. They were in truth like the eyes of a dead man, not blind, but staring, unfocused, unseeing."

Zora Neale Hurston, another U.S. writer, visited Haiti in the 1930s. She wrote about zombies in great detail. Hurston did not believe in zombies. But she was interested in Caribbean folklore and traditions. One of her zombie stories concerned a young man from the Haitian city of Cap Haitien. About thirty years earlier, he had angered his girl-friend's family, and he died soon afterward. Weeks after the death, how-ever, his mother "saw some laborers loading ox carts with bags of coffee and was astonished to see her son among those silent workers. . . . She rushed up to him screaming out his name. He regarded her without recognition and without sound." The workers' boss made the mother leave. Refusing to give up, she went for help. But by the time she returned, her son was gone. And the boss insisted that he had never seen anyone fitting the son's description. Though the mother searched and searched, she never saw her son again. She was certain, though, that she had seen her son—and that he had been made into a zombie.

Hurston reported on other zombies, including a woman named Felicia Felix-Mentor. She had died in 1907. Twenty-nine years later, in 1936, a naked woman appeared at a family farm. She claimed that she used to live

Zora Neale Hurston *(left)* learned voodoo chants and dances during her travels. Her knowledge of anthropology, the study of human biology, culture, and history, shaped her stories.

Zora Neale Hurston took this picture of Felicia Felix-Mentor (*above*) for her 1938 book *Tell My Horse*. Hurston met Felicia at a Haitian hospital, where her family had brought her to be treated for eye infections and illnesses related to starvation.

there. The owner of the farm recognized the woman as his long-dead sister. The woman's husband confirmed the identification. Hurston visited with the woman at a hospital. "The sight was dreadful," Hurston wrote. "That blank face with the dead eyes. The eyelids were white all around the eyes as if they had been burned with acid.... There was nothing you could say to her or get from her except by looking at her, and the sight of this wreckage was too much to endure for long."

Hurston also wrote about a girl named Marie. She had supposedly died in 1909. Five years later, though, friends reported seeing her. To find out the truth, people dug up her coffin. They found a skeleton inside. But the skeleton was too big for the coffin—and therefore was not Marie's. The story went on to say that Marie had become a zombie and had been forced to serve as the slave of a sorcerer. After the sorcerer died, Marie served as a slave to a Catholic priest.

Legend has it that her family finally smuggled her out of Haiti. She went to France, where she lived the rest of her life in a religious community.

According to Haitian folklore, feeding salt to a zombie will restore the person to freedom. That doesn't mean the zombie will become a living person again. Instead, the body will return to the grave.

Somewhat more recently, another zombie case made headlines. It concerned a Haitian farmer named Clairvius Narcisse. He entered a hospital in April 1962, complaining of various illnesses. Despite doctors' best efforts, he soon died. Or did he? Eighteen years later, in 1980, his sister Angelina found him wandering through their town. He claimed to have been dead for only a short time. He said that a bokor, working for their evil brother, had turned him into a zombie. For two years, Narcisse had worked as a farm slave until he was able to escape. For the next sixteen years, he had worked at odd jobs. He finally returned home after the evil brother died. When asked about his childhood, Narcisse gave all the right answers—answers that no one but the real Clairvius Narcisse could have known. That proved he wasn't an impostor. Did it prove he had been a zombie? Maybe or maybe not.

SCIENTISTS TAKE A LOOK

These stories and others have led scientists to ask questions. Even if zombies aren't real, perhaps people can enter an altered state that makes them seem like zombies. Some drugs can put people into a zombielike state. Perhaps so-called zombies are people who have been drugged. Or perhaps they are mentally ill. Mental illness can sometimes cause people to act strangely and to forget who they are or where they live.

In the 1980s, a scientist named Wade Davis set out to learn the truth about zombies in Haiti. He called his study the Zombie Project. Davis focused on the puffer fish, one of the ingredients used in voodoo to make zombies. The bodies of puffer fish contain a poison called tetrodotoxin. People who ingest (take in) just a small amount of the poison will feel light-headed. Those who take in even more may become unable to move. Victims can appear to be dead (some actually do die). Davis thought that tetrodotoxin might

Another name for a puffer fish is *fugu*. In Japan, fugu is considered a delicacy—a rare and special food. The fish (*above*) is served raw. Before serving, the chef must remove most of the tetrodotoxin from the fish. Otherwise, people who eat fugu might die.

be creating victims who looked and acted like zombies. Other scientists disagree, however, and the truth has yet to be determined for sure.

Spotlight on Zombies

Over the years, people have written stories about zombies. Zombies have also appeared in movies, TV shows, and comic books. People even play zombie computer games. The first stories about zombies involved voodoo or magic.

But times change, and so have zombies. More recently, radiation, chemicals, and aliens from outer space have all led to tales about zombie outbreaks.

PUBLISH AND PERISH

It's fairly certain that zombies don't read. But that doesn't mean other people can't read about them. In fact, zombies are central characters in a number of adventure stories.

In the 1968 film, Night of the Living Dead, radiation from outer space turned people into flesh-eating zombies.

Zombies first appeared in print in William Seabrook's *The Magic Island* (1929). The book tells about Seabrook's travels in Haiti—and his encounters with voodoo, magic, and zombies.

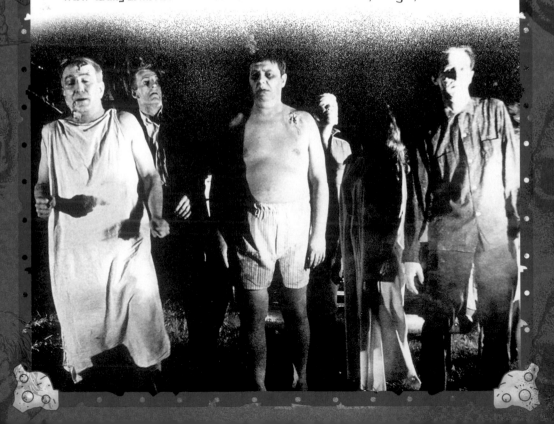

Author Zora Neale Hurston visited Jamaica. This photo from the early 1900s shows tobacco farmers like the ones she interviewed for one of her books about voodoo.

Zora Neale Hurston is best known for her novels about African American life in the early 1900s. She also wrote *Tell My Horse: Voodoo and Life in Haiti and Jamaica* (1938). This nonfiction book details Hurston's experiences in the two Caribbean nations. The people she writes about are ordinary in every way—except that they say that someone close to them became a zombie.

Other books about zombies are novels. One is *The Black Cauldron* (1965) by Lloyd Alexander. The cauldron of the title is a big black iron pot. When dead bodies are placed in it, they emerge as zombie warriors under the command of the evil Arawn. The quest of young Taran, the book's hero, is to destroy the cauldron. Not surprisingly, this is difficult to do.

In 1965 Frank Herbert wrote a book of science fiction called *Dune,* followed by other books in the Dune series. The novels are set in the future on distant planets. In Herbert's make-believe world, cells from dead people can be placed in tanks and grown into replicas, or exact copies, of the formerly living people. These zombie clones are known as gholas. Like other zombies, they have no memories of their former selves. Naturally, gholas are very useful to their masters. Should one be destroyed, another can be grown to take its place.

A British rock group from the 1960s called itself the Zombies. The group had a number of hit songs, including "She's Not There" and "Tell Her No."

The Xanth series of books of fiction was written by Piers Anthony starting in 1977 (the series has thirty-one books so far). In this series, Jonathan the Zombie Master controls the zombies. The bad news is that Jonathan can turn any dead person or animal into a zombie. The good news is that if a living person falls in love with a zombie (and the zombie loves that person in return), then the zombie can become almost alive again.

Zombies have inspired artists. Hector Hyppolite, a Haitian painter, created *The Zombies (above)* in 1946 to show the mysteries of voodoo.

In the novel *The Drum, the Doll, and the Zombie* (1994), by John Bellairs and Brad Strickland, the fearless Johnny Dixon fights for good with the help of Professor Childermass. The evil Madame Sinestra has come from Haiti to the United States with her zombie servants. She is searching for a special drum, and she has no intention of letting Johnny

get in her way. If he does, then Madame Sinestra may take revenge on Johnny's innocent grandmother.

Captain Underpants and the Invasion of the Incredibly Naughty Cafeteria Ladies from Outer Space (and the Subsequent Assault of the Equally Evil Lunchroom Zombie Nerds), by Dav Pilkey, came out in 1999. In this book, fictional fourth graders George and Harold discover that the three cafeteria workers at their school are actually evil aliens. When the boys find out that the women have plotted to turn all the students into zombie nerds, it's time for Captain Underpants to step in.

Stephen King *(above)* dedicated his book *Cell* to George Romero, who directed a series of popular zombie movies starting with *Night of the Living Dead* (1968).

Almost everything magical under the sun appears in the Harry Potter books, and zombies are no exception. In *Harry Potter and the Half-Blood Prince* (2005), the Inferi are zombies that do the bidding of the evil wizard Lord Voldemort.

Horror writer Stephen King has explored just about every sort of monster in his novels. His take on zombies shows up in his 2006 book *Cell*. In this case, it's not magic that turns people into zombies—it's cell phones. The phones wipe users' brains clean and turn them into killers. Those without cell phones are called normies. They must battle the "phoners" for survival.

THE BIG SCREEN

Early on, zombies showed up in movies. *The Cabinet of Dr. Caligari* dates to 1919. This German film features Cesare, a white-faced creature controlled by the mad Dr. Caligari. Cesare isn't called a zombie in the movie, but there's no mistaking his zombie traits. He looks like a walking corpse, and he moves in the familiar zombie shuffle.

The first American movie with the word *zombie* in the title was *White Zombie* (1932). It is a tale of love and adventure. Neil Parker and Madeleine Short have been invited to Haiti. They are to be married at the home of a friend, Charles Beaumont. What the young couple doesn't realize is that Charles is in love with Madeleine and wants her for his wife. When she refuses him, he hatches a plan. He asks a local sorcerer to fake Madeleine's death. Once Neil leaves, Charles plans to revive Madeleine and try to win her love. But the sorcerer has his own plans for Madeleine.

In *The Cabinet of Dr. Caligari* (1919), the doctor *(right)* controls the zombielike Cesare *(left)*.

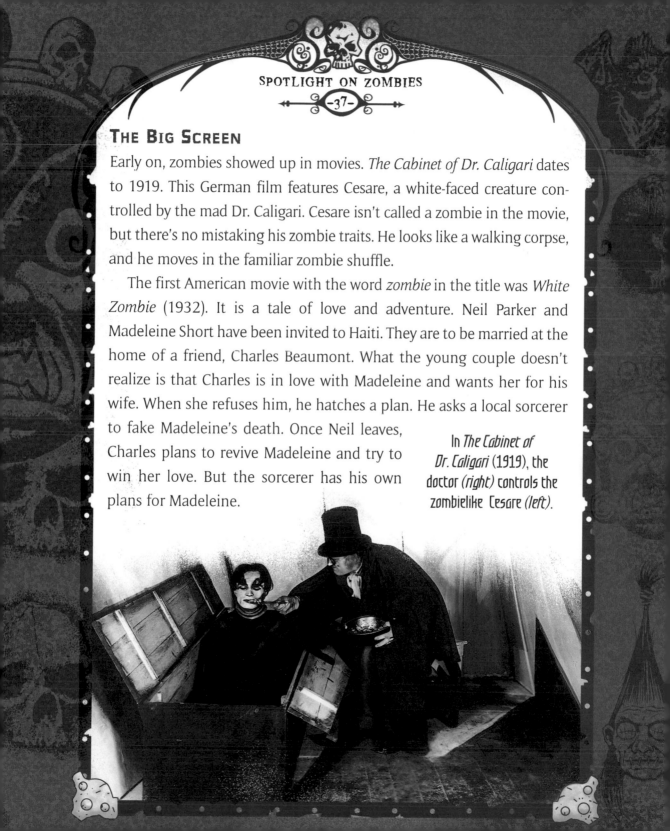

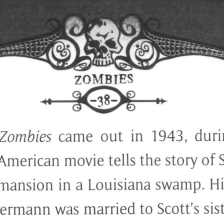

Revenge of the Zombies came out in 1943, during World War II (1939–1945). This American movie tells the story of Scott Warrington. He visits a spooky mansion in a Louisiana swamp. His host is Dr. Max von Altermann. Altermann was married to Scott's sister, Lila, until her recent death. But the doctor is up to no good. He is creating zombies to serve the Nazi army of Germany—a U.S. enemy during the war. Not only that, but Lila is one of his zombies. Even as a zombie, Lila remains stubborn enough to resist Altermann's orders.

None of the early zombie movies featured zombies ripping apart and eating human flesh. Zombies acquired that habit in later films. If one

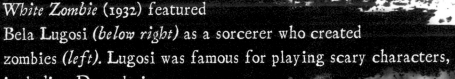

White Zombie (1932) featured
Bela Lugosi *(below right)* as a sorcerer who created
zombies *(left)*. Lugosi was famous for playing scary characters,
including Dracula in 1931.

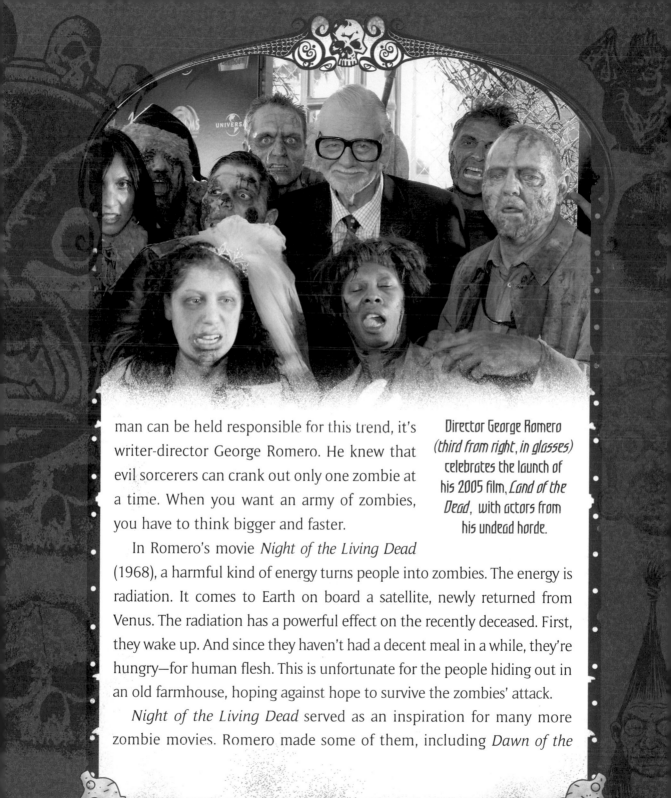

man can be held responsible for this trend, it's writer-director George Romero. He knew that evil sorcerers can crank out only one zombie at a time. When you want an army of zombies, you have to think bigger and faster.

Director George Romero (third from right, in glasses) celebrates the launch of his 2005 film, *Land of the Dead*, with actors from his undead horde.

In Romero's movie *Night of the Living Dead* (1968), a harmful kind of energy turns people into zombies. The energy is radiation. It comes to Earth on board a satellite, newly returned from Venus. The radiation has a powerful effect on the recently deceased. First, they wake up. And since they haven't had a decent meal in a while, they're hungry—for human flesh. This is unfortunate for the people hiding out in an old farmhouse, hoping against hope to survive the zombies' attack.

Night of the Living Dead served as an inspiration for many more zombie movies. Romero made some of them, including *Dawn of the*

Dead (1978). In this film, anyone who dies for any reason—car crash, heart attack, you name it—turns into a zombie.

Television has embraced zombies for many years. *Buffy the Vampire Slayer*, *South Park*, *The Simpsons*, and other popular shows have all portrayed zombies.

In the movie *Night of the Comet* (1984), two teenage girls discover one morning that almost everyone else has become a zombie overnight. The transformation happened when Earth passed through the dust of Halley's comet. (The girls were not affected because they were surrounded by protective steel.) They band together with a few other survivors to develop a drug that can save the human race. Meanwhile, hordes of hungry zombies pursue them.

The problem is much the same in the film *28 Days Later* (2003). A fast-spreading virus has turned almost all the human population into zombies. This comes as a surprise to a bicycle messenger named Jim. He awakens from a coma to find himself in a living nightmare. Naturally, Jim finds a few nonzombie companions. The question is: how long can they survive?

Survival and *zombies* are two words that are often linked. In *Shaun of the Dead* (2004), Shaun has lots of problems. He has problems at work.

ZOMBIE MOVIE MADNESS

Sometimes, the best thing about a zombie movie
is its title. Here are some examples:

American Zombie

The Astro-Zombies

Interview with a Zombie

I Walked with a Zombie

I Was a Teenage Zombie

King of the Zombies

Revolt of the Zombies

Teenage Zombies

Undead

Zombie Army

Zombie Bloodbath

The Zombie Chronicles

Zombie Honeymoon

Zombie Hunger

Zombie Island Massacre

Zombie Planet

Zombie Prom

Zombies of the Stratosphere

"ATTACK OF THE ZOMBIE COMPUTERS"

In 2007 U.S. newspapers reported that an army of zombies was committing crimes. Was this zombie attack for real? It sure was. But the zombies were not the "undead." Instead, they were personal computers. People had programmed the computers to commit Internet crimes, such as stealing credit card numbers from other computers. Just like zombies in books and movies, computer zombies are mindless robots. Criminal programmers take them over and tell them what to do.

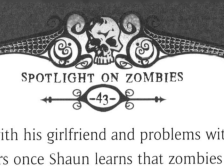

He has problems with his girlfriend and problems with his family. But none of this matters once Shaun learns that zombies are roaming the streets of London. If Shaun is going to save himself and the ones he loves, he is going to have to get off the couch and become a hero.

As these films illustrate, when the going gets tough with zombies, it's best to get going yourself—as far away as possible. It's bad enough to be killed by a monster. But with zombies, you don't just get killed—you become a zombie meal. Or you might even become a zombie yourself. To avoid this fate, pay attention to any creatures that may be lurching in your direction. Should you see one, don't reach out a helping hand—you might not get it back.

Dozens of hungry zombies reach for a victim in the 2004 movie *Shaun of the Dead*.

Source Notes

26 Daniel Farson, *Vampires, Zombies, and Monster Men* (Garden City, NY: Doubleday and Company, 1976), 66.

27 Zora Neale Hurston, *Folklore, Memoirs and Other Writings* (New York: Library of America, 1995), 466–467.

28 Ibid., 469.

Selected Bibliography

Cohen, Daniel. *Voodoo, Devils and the New Invisible World.* New York: Dodd, Mead and Company, 1972.

Farson, Daniel. *Vampires, Zombies, and Monster Men.* Garden City, NY: Doubleday and Company, 1976.

Hurston, Zora Neale. *Folklore, Memoirs and Other Writings.* New York: Library of America, 1995.

Kristos, Kyle. *Voodoo.* New York: J. B. Lippincott Company, 1976.

Further Reading and Websites

Alexander, Lloyd. *The Black Cauldron.* New York: Henry Holt and Company, 1965. Taran must destroy a black cauldron that can bring people back from the dead to serve as zombie soldiers.

Bellairs, John, and Brad Strickland. *The Drum, the Doll, and the Zombie.* New York: Dial Books, 1994. Young Johnny Dixon and his friend Professor Childermass battle evil in the form of voodoo priestess Madame Sinestra from Haiti. She is up to no good, and Johnny must stop her dastardly scheme to increase her power.

Brooks, Max. *The Zombie Survival Guide.* New York: Three Rivers Press, 2003. This book tells everything you ever wanted to know about zombies—how to defend yourself from zombies, the best places to hide

out when necessary, and, most importantly, how to avoid becoming a zombie yourself.

Herbert, Frank. *Dune*. New York: Berkley Books, 1977. This work of science fiction centers on the adventures of Paul Atreides and his experiences on the planet Arrakis. In the complex story, zombies are just one of Paul's many problems.

Herbst, Judith. *Monsters*. Minneapolis: Lerner Publications, 2004. This book features five different monsters, including zombies. It examines the stories about and evidence of each monster and asks whether or not they really exist.

Hurston, Zora Neale. *Tell My Horse: Voodoo and Life in Haiti and Jamaica*. Philadelphia: J. B. Lippincott, 1938. This nonfiction book explores life in Haiti and Jamaica in the mid-1900s. Hurston includes several dramatic examples of people believed to be zombies.

I Love Zombies Page
http://www.zombiejuice.com
If you love zombies or want to learn more about them, this site is a good place to start. It contains zombie resources from the worlds of print, movies, and other media.

Kallen, Stuart. *Voodoo*. San Diego: Lucent Books, 2005. The author examines voodoo, a Haitian religious practice with roots in Africa. Zombie making is just one small part of this fascinating tradition.

Rowling, J. K. *Harry Potter and the Half-Blood Prince*. New York: Scholastic, 2005. In the sixth book in the Harry Potter series, Harry is still fighting the evil wizard Voldemort. Harry has his friends to help him, but Voldemort has many servants, including the zombielike Inferi.

MOVIES

Cabinet of Dr. Caligari, The. DVD. Chatsworth, CA: Image Entertainment, 1997.

This film from the silent era features the zombielike Cesare and the evil Dr. Caligari. The movie was made in 1919, before zombie movies became horror classics.

Ghost Breakers, The. DVD. Universal City, CA: Universal Studios, 2002.

A zombie, a ghost, and other scary creatures join beloved actors Bob Hope and Paulette Goddard in this 1941 comedy.

Revolt of the Zombies, The. DVD. Union, NJ: Madacy Entertainment, 1998.

In this chiller from 1936, a secret formula holds the key to turning people into zombies. Who will discover the secret first?

White Zombie. DVD. Orlando, FL: A27CDS, 2005.

This movie classic, starring Bela Lugosi, put the scare into audiences when it came out in theaters in 1932. Zombie movies have since become a lot scarier.

INDEX

About the Author

Stephen Krensky is the author of many fiction and nonfiction books for children, including titles in the On My Own Folklore series and *Bigfoot*, *The Bogeyman*, *Dragons*, *Frankenstein*, *Ghosts*, *The Mummy*, *Vampires*, *Watchers in the Woods*, *Werewolves*, and *Zombies*. When he isn't hunched over his computer, he makes school visits and teaches writing workshops. In his free time, he enjoys playing tennis and softball and reading books by other people. Krensky lives in Massachusetts with his wife, Joan, and their family.

Photo Acknowledgments